LANDMARK TOP TENS

The World's Most Amazing
Monuments

Ann Weil

Chicago, Illinois

www.heinemannraintree.com
Visit our website to find out
more information about
Heinemann-Raintree books.

To order:
☎ Phone 888-454-2279
▣ Visit www.heinemannraintree.com
to browse our catalog and order online.

© 2012 Raintree
an imprint of Capstone Global Library, LLC
Chicago, Illinois

Customer Service: 888-454-2279
Visit our website at www.heinemannraintree.com

Edited by Megan Cotugno and Vaarunika Dharmapala
Designed by Victoria Allen
Picture research by Hannah Taylor and Ruth Blair
Illustrated by HL Studios and Oxford Designers
    and Illustrators
Original illustrations © Capstone Global Library Ltd (2011)
Production by Camilla Crask
Originated by Capstone Global Library Ltd
Printed in China by CTPS

15 14 13 12 11
10 9 8 7 6 5 4 3 2 1

Library of Congress Cataloging-in-Publication Data
Weil, Ann.
  The world's most amazing monuments / Ann Weil. —1st ed.
     p. cm.—(Landmark top tens)
  Includes bibliographical references and index.
  ISBN 978-1-4109-4236-4 (hc)—ISBN 978-1-4109-4247-
0 (pbk.) 1. Monuments—Juvenile literature. 2. Cultural
property—Protection—Juvenile literature. I. Title.
  CC135.W395 2011
  363.6'9—dc22   2010038395

Acknowledgments
The author and publishers are grateful to the following for
permission to reproduce copyright material: Alamy Images
pp. 16 (© GlowImages), 20 (© Andrew Gransden), 21
(© RIA Novosti); FLPA p. 7 (Minden Pictures/Konrad Wothe);
Getty Images pp. 9 (AFP), 19 (Popperfoto/Bob Thomas), 24
(Travel Ink), 27 (AFP PHOTO/INDRANIL MUKHERJEE);
Photolibrary p. 26 (DEA); Photoshot p. 23 (Newscom);
Shutterstock pp. 4 (© Paul Prescott), 5 (© naipung), 6 (© David
Evison), 8 (© sashagala), 10 (© Jonathan Larsen), 12 (© niall
dunne), 14 (© Matthew Jacques), 18 (© Mike Norton), 22
(© Mark Schwettmann); The Art Archive p. 17 (Musée du
Louvre Paris/Dagli Orti).

Cover photograph of giant monolithic stone Moai statues
at Rano Raraku, Rapa Nui (Easter Island) reproduced with
permission of Photolibrary (Robert Harding).

We would like to thank Daniel Block for his invaluable help in
the preparation of this book.

Contents

Monuments 4

Taj Mahal 6

Brandenburg Gate 8

Mount Rushmore 10

The Moai of Easter Island 12

Stonehenge 14

Great Sphinx of Giza 16

Devils Tower 18

The Motherland 20

Statue of Christ the Redeemer 22

Great Ocean Road 24

Monuments in Danger 26

Monuments Facts and Figures *28*

Glossary *30*

Find Out More *31*

Index *32*

Some words are printed in bold, **like this**. You can find out
what they mean in the glossary.

Monuments

Statues, buildings and even natural features can be monuments. A monument honors an important person or event. Some monuments celebrate freedom. Others pay tribute to historical figures such as kings, queens, or presidents. Some monuments, such as tombstones, are small and personal. Others are built on a large scale, such as the Statue of Liberty in New York City harbor.

This statue in New Delhi, India, is a monument to Mohandas (Mahatma) Gandhi (1869–1948). He showed the people of India, and the world, that nonviolent protest was an effective way to win freedom.

Monument mysteries

Some monuments were created so long ago that people today no longer remember why they were built. These monuments from **antiquity** remain a mystery. Visitors to amazing monuments such as Stonehenge in England can only guess at what they meant to those who created them.

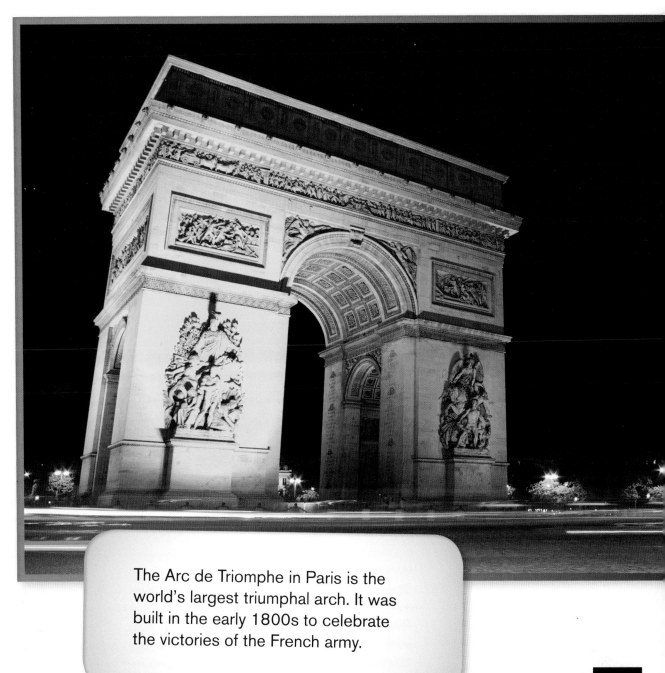

The Arc de Triomphe in Paris is the world's largest triumphal arch. It was built in the early 1800s to celebrate the victories of the French army.

Taj Mahal

In 1607 an emperor of India and a Persian princess fell in love. She was only 14 years old. Five years later they were married.

Taj Mahal
Location: Agra, Utter Pradesh, India
Size: 213 feet (65 meters) high at the center of the dome
That's Amazing!
This beautiful building is actually a **tomb**!

Construction of this incredible monument began in 1631. It took more than 20,000 workers over 20 years to build.

The Taj Mahal was built using elephant labor. More than 1,000 elephants helped move building materials.

The Seven Wonders of the World

In 2007, the Taj Mahal became one of the new **Seven Wonders of the World**. People voted online for 21 sites. More than 90 million votes were cast.

Tragedy strikes

In 1631 the emperor's wife died giving birth to their 14th child. The heartbroken emperor designed the world's most beautiful monument in honor of his beloved wife. Although separated by her death, their bodies now lie together in this amazing **mausoleum**.

Brandenburg Gate

The Brandenburg Gate was created as a monument to peace in the late 1700s. This was the King of Prussia's idea. But his monument did not remain as a symbol of peace.

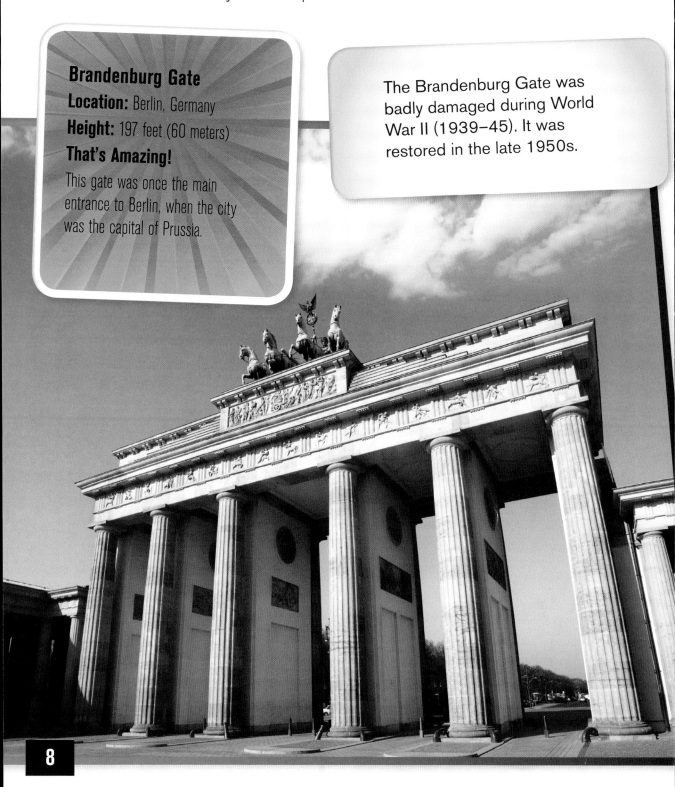

Brandenburg Gate

Location: Berlin, Germany

Height: 197 feet (60 meters)

That's Amazing!

This gate was once the main entrance to Berlin, when the city was the capital of Prussia.

The Brandenburg Gate was badly damaged during World War II (1939–45). It was restored in the late 1950s.

Germany: divided and reunited

In the 1960s the gate became part of the Berlin Wall. It was a symbol of a country divided in two. The **Communist** government of East Germany built the wall to stop its citizens from escaping to West Germany. When the wall came down in 1989 and the two countries were reunited, the Brandenburg Gate was once again a symbol of peace and unity.

The gate was closed for almost 30 years (1961–89) when Germany was a divided country. It reopened after the Berlin Wall came down.

Mount Rushmore

There are many monuments to presidents of the United States, but Mount Rushmore is the most famous. The heads of Presidents George Washington, Thomas Jefferson, Theodore Roosevelt, and Abraham Lincoln are carved into the side of a mountain.

Mount Rushmore

Location: South Dakota, USA

Height: Each head is about 60 feet (18 meters) high

That's Amazing!

Early plans for this monument included the presidents' chests as well as their heads, but they were not finished.

Each president's head is about 60 feet (18 meters) tall, which is as high as a 6-story building!

Building this monument cost as much as constructing a skyscraper in those days. The total cost was nearly $1 million.

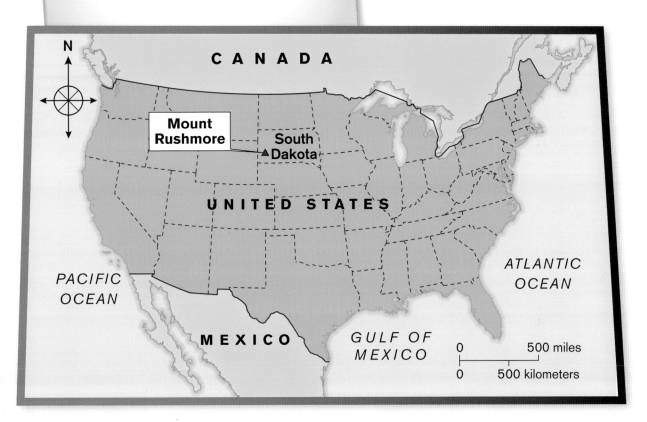

Blasting a mountain

Creating this monument was hard and dangerous work. It was started in 1927 and took 400 workers more than 14 years to complete. First, dynamite was used to blast off the top layers of rock. Then workers hanging off the side of the mountain used small tools to carve the granite that lay underneath. It is amazing that not one worker died during the construction!

The Moai of Easter Island

There are nearly 900 statues on Easter Island. Each shows the head and upper body of a man. The people who live on the island now call them "Moai." But even they do not know for certain who, or what, these statues **commemorate**. Experts think the Moai represent the spirits of **ancestors** or other important people from the island.

These stone giants were created about 500–700 years ago.

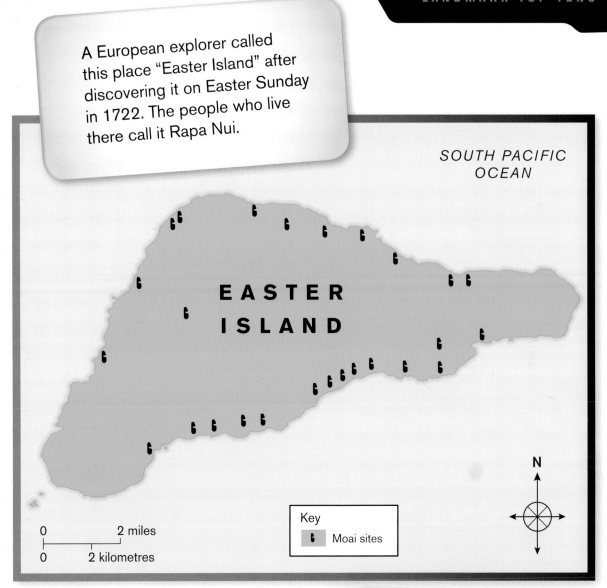

A European explorer called this place "Easter Island" after discovering it on Easter Sunday in 1722. The people who live there call it Rapa Nui.

SOUTH PACIFIC OCEAN

EASTER ISLAND

0 — 2 miles
0 — 2 kilometres

Key
🗿 Moai sites

N

Unfinished business

Some experts think the people abandoned their project unfinished. Or maybe the statues were left near roads on purpose. Either way, how people moved these huge, heavy stone monuments is still one of the world's unsolved mysteries.

The Moai of Easter Island

Location: Easter Island, in the southeast Pacific Ocean (part of Chile)

Statue Height: Up to 40 feet (12 meters)

That's Amazing!

Although these monuments are among the most famous in the world, they are the least visited because of their remote location.

Stonehenge

Scientists believe that ancient people built Stonehenge about 4,600 years ago. But no one knows exactly how or why they moved the 25- to 49-ton sandstone blocks into place. There is no written history to guide us. Legends offer fantastic explanations that are hard to believe. One tells how Merlin, the wizard in the King Arthur legend, created Stonehenge using magic.

Archaeologists believe there was an older, wooden version of Stonehenge. Over many years, the timbers were replaced with stone.

Stonehenge

Location: Salisbury Plain, United Kingdom

Height of tallest piece: 22 feet (7 meters)

That's Amazing!

Stonehenge is the most famous prehistoric site in Europe.

Ancient astronomy

Ancient people were as fascinated as we are today by the movements of the stars and planets in the night sky. But they lacked telescopes and other modern tools to help them learn more. Stonehenge may have been an ancient **observatory**.

This is a plan of how Stonehenge may have looked. Experts think there was an outer circle of stones, with an inner row arranged in a horseshoe pattern.

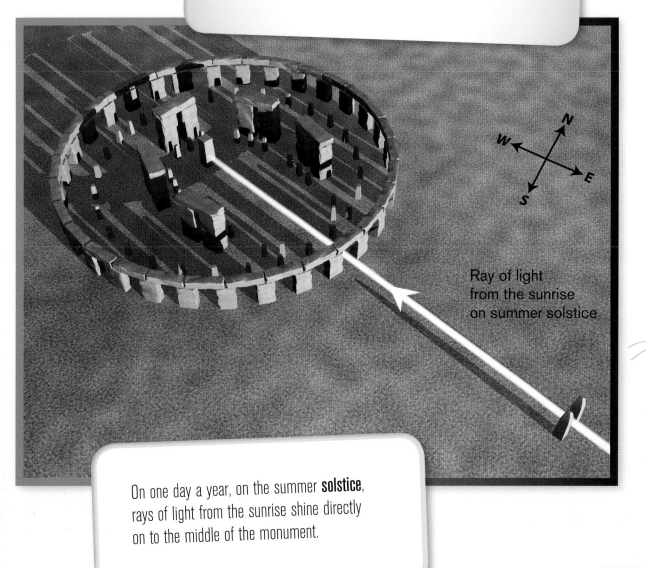

Ray of light from the sunrise on summer solstice

On one day a year, on the summer **solstice**, rays of light from the sunrise shine directly on to the middle of the monument.

Great Sphinx of Giza

The Great Sphinx of Giza has the head of a human on the body of a lion. Ancient Egyptians carved the Sphinx from a natural outcrop of rock. The paws were made from stone blocks. In ancient times, the face and body were painted red. The headdress was yellow with blue stripes.

Great Sphinx of Giza
Location: Egypt
Size: 66 feet (20 meters) tall; 240 feet (73 meters) long
That's Amazing!
The Sphinx represents two Egyptian gods—the **pharaoh** god and the lion god.

Experts believe that the Sphinx was built between 2558 and 2532 BCE.

Shifting sands

At times the Sphinx was buried up to its neck in sand! A legend tells of an Egyptian prince who slept in the statue's shadow. He dreamed that the Sphinx offered to make him king instead of his older brother if he promised to clear the sand around the statue. The prince agreed and became King Thutmose IV.

This is a statue of King Thutmose IV. Some historians think he made his story up after killing his brother. He thought that people might forgive the murder if it was the will of the gods.

Devils Tower

This natural feature is **sacred** to Native Americans. They call it Mateo Teepee, which means Bear Lodge. Legends tell of how this unusual rock got its name. In one story, a bear was chasing some girls. They jumped onto a low rock and begged the rock to save them. The rock grew taller with the girls still on top!

Monuments reflect what is important to the people who create them. Devils Tower National Monument shows how Americans value their natural **heritage**.

Devils Tower
Location: Black Hills, Wyoming, USA
Height: 867 feet (264 meters)
That's Amazing!
Devils Tower is acually the core of an ancient volcano.

Stuck on Devils Tower!

In 1941 a man had a risky idea for a stunt. He parachuted safely onto the top of Devils Tower. But the rope he needed to climb down landed on the side of the rock. He could not reach it. Food and blankets were dropped to keep him alive until he was rescued six days later.

In 1906 U.S. President Theodore Roosevelt (seen here) declared Devils Tower the country's first national monument.

The Motherland

This amazing monument has many names: the Motherland, Mother Motherland, and the Motherland Calls. It was built to honor Russian soldiers who fought **Nazi** forces in the Battle of Stalingrad during World War II. Russia was on the side of the Allies. This was a group of nations fighting together against the Nazis, including the United Kingdom and the United States.

History often plays down the Russian contribution to victory in World War II. This monument **commemorates** the Russian soldiers' bravery, **sacrifice**, and victory.

The Battle of Stalingrad was the bloodiest in human history. Much of the city was destroyed, and 2 million people were killed or seriously wounded.

Winning the battle and the war

The Russians won the battle, which was a major turning point in the war. If the Nazis had taken the Russian city of Stalingrad, they could have controlled Russia, and the war might have ended differently.

The Motherland

Location: Volgograd, Russia

Size: 279 feet (85 meters) from the tip of its sword to the top of the plinth (pedestal)

That's Amazing!

It is one of the tallest statues in the world!

Statue of Christ the Redeemer

Above the harbor city of Rio de Janeiro in Brazil towers the world-famous statue of Christ the Redeemer. In the mid-1800s a Brazilian **Catholic** priest first had the idea for placing a **Christian** monument on the top of the 2,310-foot (704-meter) high Mount Corcovado. It took more than 60 years for the idea to became a reality.

Statue of Christ the Redeemer

Location: Rio de Janeiro, Brazil
Height: 98.5 feet (30 meters)

That's Amazing!
In 2007 the statue was officially chosen as one of the New Seven Wonders of the World.

A lightning strike!

Designed as a symbol of peace, the statue is 98.5 feet
(30 meters) high and took more than five years to construct.
It was finally unveiled to the public in October 1931. Then, in
2008, a violent storm hit Rio de Janeiro, uprooting trees and
destroying buildings. People feared that the statue would be
destroyed. It was struck by lightning, but survived with only
minor damage to the face and fingers.

This amazing photograph was
taken at the moment that the
statue was struck by lightning.

Great Ocean Road

War memorials pay tribute to soldiers who fought and died for their country. The Great Ocean Road is an amazing war memorial in Australia. It is a road built by soldiers in memory of their fallen comrades in World War I (1914–18).

This scenic road runs alongside the Southern Ocean, past unusual rock formations that dot the coastline.

ANZAC Day

Every year on the April 25, people in Australia and New Zealand pay tribute to soldiers who died serving their country. ANZAC stands for Australia and New Zealand Army Corps. ANZAC Day began as a memorial to soldiers who fought in the battle at Gallipoli, Turkey, during World War I.

The Great Ocean Road is a popular tourist route, with towns, national parks, and beaches along the way.

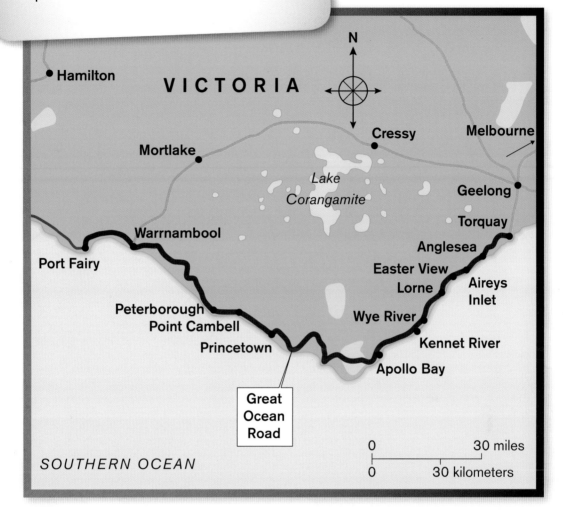

Building the road

Workers used dynamite to blow out rocks in the road's path. About 3,000 men used picks and shovels to clear the road. They lived in camps set up in the bush along the route. Making the road was hard, dangerous work. Several men died during its construction.

Great Ocean Road
Location: Australia
Length: 163 miles (263 kilometers)
That's Amazing!
It is the world's largest war memorial.

Monuments in Danger

Many existing monuments are in danger. Natural disasters, such as earthquakes, destroy monuments. In 2007 an earthquake in Peru badly damaged hundreds of monuments. There may not be enough money to rebuild and restore them. Some monuments are destroyed on purpose.

This standing Buddha was carved into the side of a cliff in the Bamiyan Valley, in what is now central Afghanistan.

Bamiyan Buddha

A statue known as the Bamiyan Buddha watched over **caravans** moving along the **Silk Road** to and from China from around 554 CE. At that time, many people who lived and traveled through the Bamiyan Valley were **Buddhists**.

In 2001 a religious group known as the Taliban controlled Afghanistan. The Taliban are **Muslims** and wanted only Islamic objects in their country. So they blew up the Bamiyan Buddha.

One of the men involved in the destruction of the Buddha said: "All we are breaking is stones."

Monuments Facts and Figures

There are millions of monuments all over the world. They are different shapes and sizes and are made of different materials. But they all have one thing in common. They help us to remember something or someone important. Which monument do you think is the most amazing?

Taj Mahal

Location: Agra, Utter Pradesh, India

Size: 213 feet (65 meters) high at the center of the dome

That's Amazing!

This beautiful building is actually a **tomb**!

Brandenburg Gate

Location: Berlin, Germany

Height: 197 feet (60 meters)

That's Amazing!

This gate was once the main entrance to Berlin, when the city was the capital of Prussia.

Mount Rushmore

Location: South Dakota, USA

Height: Each head is about 60 feet (18 meters) high

That's Amazing!

Early plans for this monument included the presidents' chests as well as their heads—but they were not finished.

The Moai of Easter Island

Location: Easter Island, in the southeast Pacific Ocean (part of Chile)

Statue Height: Up to 40 feet (12 meters)

That's Amazing!

Although these monuments are among the most famous in the world, they are the least visited because of their remote location.

Stonehenge

Location: Salisbury Plain, United Kingdom

Height of tallest piece: 22 feet (7 meters)

That's Amazing!

Stonehenge is the most famous prehistoric site in Europe.

Great Sphinx of Giza

Location: Egypt

Size: 66 feet (20 meters) tall; 240 feet (73 meters) long

That's Amazing!

The Sphinx represents two Egyptian gods—the **pharaoh** god and the lion god.

Devils Tower

Location: Black Hills, Wyoming, USA

Height: 867 feet (264 meters)

That's Amazing!

Devils Tower is acually the core of an ancient volcano.

The Motherland

Location: Volgograd, Russia

Size: 279 feet (85 meters) from the tip of its sword to the top of the plinth (pedestal)

That's Amazing!

It is one of the tallest statues in the world!

Statue of Christ the Redeemer

Location: Rio de Janeiro, Brazil

Height: 98.5 feet (30 meters)

That's Amazing!

In 2007 the statue was officially chosen as one of the New Seven Wonders of the World.

Great Ocean Road

Location: Australia

Length: 163 miles (263 kilometers)

That's Amazing!

It is the world's largest war memorial.

Glossary

ancestors grandparents, great-grandparents, and other relatives who lived a long time ago

antiquity ancient times, a very long time ago

archaeologist someone who studies ancient remains

Buddhist person who follows the world religion of Buddhism that originated in India around 500 BCE

caravan group of people with animals (usually horses or camels) that travels from one place to another to trade goods

Catholic belonging to the Christian Roman Catholic Church

Christian person who follows the teachings of Jesus Christ

citizen person who has the legal right to live in a country or state

commemorate to honor, remember, or celebrate something or someone important

Communist kind of government that puts public needs before private rights

heritage history and places from the past valued by future generations

mausoleum building that contains one or more tombs

Muslim person who is a follower of the world religion of Islam

Nazi someone associated with a political party in Germany led by Adolf Hitler in the 1930s and early 1940s

observatory place constructed for the purpose of watching and learning about stars and planets

pharaoh a king in ancient Egypt

relic something from a long time ago that survived when the rest was destroyed

sacred connected with religion

sacrifice give up something valuable, such as one's own life

Seven Wonders of the World originally a list of seven ancient structures recorded by a Greek traveler more than 2,000 years ago

Silk Road ancient trade routes connecting China and Europe

solstice day of the year (in summer) when there are most hours of daylight. The winter solstice is the day of the year when there are most hours of darkness.

tomb grave, cave, or other place where a dead body is buried

Find Out More

Books

Harris, Nancy. *Mount Rushmore*. Chicago, IL: Heinemann Library, 2009.

Giblin, James. *Secrets of the Sphinx*. New York, NY: Scholastic, 2004.

Doeden, Matt. *Stonehenge*. Mankato, Minn.: Capstone, 2007.

Tagliaferro, Linda and Stephen Brown. *Taj Mahal: India's Majestic Tomb*. New York, NY: Bearport, 2005.

Websites

http://guardians.net/egypt/sphinx/
Learn more about the Sphinx and look at some amazing photos!

http://www.learningbox.com/bunny/rapanui/
Find out more about the mysterious Moai of Easter Island (Rapa Nui).

Index

Afghanistan 23, 26–27
ancestors 12
ANZAC Day 24
Arc de Triomphe 5
astronomy 15
Australia 24–25

Battle of Stalingrad 20, 21
Berlin Wall 9
Brandenburg Gate 8–9
Buddhism 26, 27
buildings 4, 6–9, 22–23

commemoration 12, 20
Communism 9
construction 7, 11, 16, 25
copper 22
costs 11, 22

destruction of monuments
    26–27
Devils Tower 18–19
dynamite 11, 25

earthquakes 26
Easter Island 12–13
Egypt 16–17
England 5, 14–15

France 5

Gandhi, Mahatma 4
Germany 8–9
Great Ocean Road 24–25
Great Sphinx of Giza
    16–17

India 4, 6–7

Jefferson, Thomas 10

legends 14, 17, 18
Lincoln, Abraham 10

mausoleum 7
Moai 12–13
The Motherland 20–21
Mount Rushmore 10–11

national monuments 19
Native Americans 18
natural features 4, 18–19
Nazis 20, 21
New Seven Wonders of
    the World 22

Rio de Janeiro 22–23
Roosevelt, Theodore 10,
    19
Russia 20–21

sacred sites 18, 22–23
Seven Wonders of the
    World 7
Silk Road 27
Statue of Christ the
    Redeemer 22–23
Statue of Liberty 4
statues 4, 12–13, 16–17,
    20–21, 22–23
Stonehenge 5, 14–15
summer solstice 15

Taj Mahal 6–7
tombstones 4

United States 4, 10–11,
    18–19

volcanoes 18

war memorials 20–21,
    24–25
Washington, George 10
World War I 24
World War II 20–21